jake's gift

jake's gift

Lest We Forget

Julia Mackey

JMackey

Jake's Gift
First published 2013 by Scirocco Drama,
an imprint of J. Gordon Shillingford Publishing Inc.
© 2013 Julia Mackey
Second printing, 2014
Third printing, 2015
Fourth printing, 2015
Fifth printing, 2017

Scirocco Drama Editor: Glenda MacFarlane
Cover photo by Julia Mackey with graphic design by Dirk Van Stralen
Cover design by Terry Gallagher/Doowah Design Inc.
Author photo by Michael Ford
Printed and bound in Canada on 100% post-consumer recycled paper.

We acknowledge the financial support of the Manitoba Arts Council and The Canada
Council for the Arts for our publishing program.

The three production photos reproduced in the book were taken during a run of *Jake's
Gift*. The production was presented at the Firehall Arts Centre in November 2008, by
the Vancouver East Cultural Centre. All three photos were taken by Tim Matheson.

Library and Archives Canada Cataloguing in Publication

Mackey, Julia, 1967-, author
    Jake's gift / Julia Mackey.

A play.
ISBN 978-1-897289-98-3 (pbk.)

    I. Title.

PS8625.K49J34 2013   C812'.6   C2013-907018-4

J. Gordon Shillingford Publishing
P.O. Box 86, RPO Corydon Avenue, Winnipeg, MB Canada R3M 3S3

For all of our veterans, past and present, this is my love letter to you and my promise to remember.

Lest We Forget.

Acknowledgements

Thank you to Antony Holland, Fred Rogers, Jan de Vries, Art Heximer, Al Mason, Bill Rowe, Don Dawson, Alan Lawrence, Chester and Clifford Hebner, George and Alice Phelps (Hebner), The Hebner Family, The Heximer Family, Ken Cavendish, Bill Ross, Doug Vidler, Bud Schaupmeyer, Robert Hay, Al Hebburn, Jack Newman, Jack Hadley, Doris Gregory, Harry Fox, Richard "Moose" Norris, Kathleen Norris, Paul Martin, Kelvin Mactier, Brian Budden, Dirk Van Stralen, Jennifer Swan, Gerald King, John Van Stralen, Tim Matheson, Karen Jeffery, Dave Jeffery, Tim Sutherland, Raelynne Gagnon, Holly Jones, James Douglas, Ian Case, Janet Munsil, Holly Vivian, David Ross, Jeremy Tow, Roy Surette, Ron Reed, Stephen Massicotte, Stephen Drover, Amiel Gladstone, Simon Johnson, Kim Collier, David Kerr, Scott Bellis, Dawn Petten, Joanna Maratta, Freda Van Stralen, Beckett Van Stralen, Walker Van Stralen, Paul Mackey, Caroline Murphy, Michael Murphy, Ken Mackey, Clare Mackey, Michael Laurette, Benjamin Laurette, Isabella Laurette and Gord Shillingford.

Director's Note

Sometimes the best way to get a look at the Big Picture is to not do so at all. If *Jake's Gift* succeeds, it is because of Julia's ability to take a lofty concept—the importance of remembrance—and make it utterly personal. This is the story of one soldier and one grave, yet it bristles with an emotional authenticity that speaks to the universal heart of loss, simply and directly. In creating the show, we wanted to reflect that simplicity. Expect no fancy projections, choreography or sound effects: this is about a person and a story. Enjoy.

—Dirk Van Stralen

Playwright's Note

In 2002, Ron Reed, Artistic Director of Pacific Theatre in Vancouver, BC, gave me the opportunity to participate in a three-week intensive mask characterization workshop. It was like nothing I had ever experienced before. It was in this workshop that I created the character of Jake. After the process finished, I couldn't quite let go of Jake, and I knew I wanted to create another project with him in mind. In late 2003, I learned that there would be a commemoration ceremony in Normandy for the 60th Anniversary of D-Day. Given the war theme I had created for Jake's story in the workshop, I had an inkling I would find the story I was looking for on the shores of Juno Beach. I called Veterans Affairs Canada, got my name on the visitors' list, and in June 2004 I travelled to Normandy, France, for the 60th Anniversary of D-Day. It was one of the most moving journeys of my life, and I felt compelled to share that experience with other Canadians. For one week, I attended ceremonies, visited graveyards, and walked the beaches and countryside. I interviewed dozens of veterans who had returned for the anniversary. For many it was their first time back since the war. Their stories were inspiring and moving, and I am forever grateful to each of them for their willingness to share them with me. *Jake's Gift* is a love letter to all veterans, and is my way of saying thank you to a generation of men and women who sacrificed much for the greater good. Every day, I become more aware of how quickly they are leaving us now. I've promised many of my 90-year-old boyfriends and girlfriends that I will keep telling their story long after they are gone. I hope to do just that.

—Julia Mackey

Characters

Jake   A cantankerous 80-year-old Canadian WW 2
                veteran.

Isabelle   A precocious 10-year-old French girl from the
                local village.

Grand-mama   Isabelle's grandmother; Grande-Isabelle, a poised
                70-year-old.

Susan   A Canadian teacher from small town Ontario. 30-
                something.

Setting

The play takes place between June 4th and June 7th, 2004 at the 60th
Anniversary of D-Day ceremonies in various settings in and around
the area of Juno Beach in Normandy, France.

The Set

Downstage left there is a French colonial style side table with a small
black typewriter case placed next to it.
Downstage right is a bench with a rectangular parcel/box placed
behind it.
References to all other set pieces in the play are imagined.

Production History

Jake's Gift had its professional premiere at Gabriola Theatre Centre, Gabriola Island, BC, on January 13, 2007 with the following cast and crew:

Written and Performed by Julia Mackey

Directed and Stage Managed by Dirk Van Stralen

In the fall of 2008, a professional lighting design was created by Gerald King, and a professional set design was created and built by John Van Stralen.

In August 2006, *Jake's Gift* received a week-long workshop and a two-night staged reading at the Sunset Theatre in Wells, BC, on August 18/20, 2006 with the following cast and crew:

Written and Performed by Julia Mackey

Directed by Tim Sutherland

Technical Director: Holly Jones

Stage Manager: Raelynne Gagnon

Photo by Michael Ford

Julia Mackey

Julia Mackey was born in Birmingham, England. When she was three years old her family moved to Canada. She grew up in Beaconsfield, Quebec. After graduating with a B.Ed from McGill University, Julia moved to Victoria, BC, to pursue a more creative life. It was there she met and trained with artist Robert Osborne, who introduced her to the world of theatre. Soon after, she started writing and performing with the acclaimed theatre troupe Theatre SKAM. In 2007, Julia and her partner and director, Dirk Van Stralen, created Juno Productions. To date, they have toured *Jake's Gift* to over 225 communities across Canada. When not on the road, Julia splits her time between Vancouver and Wells, BC.

Part 1 – Meeting on Juno Beach

> *The play starts in the black. Louis Prima's "Oh Marie" plays until "kiss me once while the stars shine above me." After that line, ISABELLE stomps her foot and the lights snap up.*

ISABELLE: My name is Isabelle and I am ten years old, and I have the most important job in the whole of the world. Well, not just me, me and my classmates. We all take care of the soldiers. We clean their rooms for them and tidy their gardens, and pull out all the weeds so that they can see through their windows.

My grand-mama says that it's a good thing that we do that. I live with my grand-mama in a small town on the coast of Normandy, France. It is called Bernières-sur-Mer, but you might know it better as Juno Beach... Ju-Know it? Ahhh... Get it? Ju-Know it? Ahhh, I like that joke. Jake told it to me. Jake is my best friend. Well, no, Jake is my best *boy* friend, but he's not my *real* boyfriend. He can't be my real boyfriend because he's too old. Besides, I already have a boyfriend, but that boy just doesn't know it yet.

I met Jake on the beach in front of my house. He's one of the soldiers that came here for the 60th Anniversary of D-Day.

Most of the days, Bernières-sur-Mer is a pretty sleepy town, but not right now. Soldiers are arriving here every day with their families for the big celebrations. The whole town is very excited, and every house and shop has the Canada flag flying. Some of the old folks in town, they remember the day the Canadians landed on Juno Beach. June 6th, 1944!

My grand-mama? She was my age when the soldiers first came here. She told me that our house was taken over by Nazi soldiers, and she had to go and live in Caen with her papa and her brother André. My grand-mama is sad sometimes. Sometimes? When we go for walks on the beach? She just holds my hand tight, and she stares out at the water and she cries.

Grand-mama, why are you crying?

GRAND-MAMA: ...Because Isabelle, when you lose someone you love that pain never goes away, and some days it sits so close to your heart that you can't help but to cry.

ISABELLE: ...Her papa was killed by a Nazi soldier. He was a French resistance fighter. He was an artist and made secret maps for the Allies to show them where the Nazis were hiding.

Lots of French resistance fighters were killed. My uncle André was a resistance fighter too, and he only survived because he was just fourteen, and my great-grandfather begged the German soldier not to kill him because he was only a child.

GRAND-MAMA: Ça-suffit Isabelle!

ISABELLE: Oui, d'accord.

Grand-mama says that everyone is especially excited about this anniversary, the 60th anniversary, because it might be the last big celebration.

GRAND-MAMA: That's because the veterans are getting old now.

Most of them are in their eighties, and it's hard for them to keep coming back here year after year.

…Voilà, you see, unh? Like that man over there.

JAKE: The last thing in the goddamn world I wanted to be was a soldier. I wanted to be a jockey, but that didn't work out, so I became a bookie instead. But that didn't work out either. Somethin' you might wanna note; when you're in the middle of a depression and the whole damn country is lookin' for work, and no one has any goddamn money to bet on the horses, then bein' a bookie is probably not your best job option. So when a war breaks out and there ain't no jobs around, it's pretty obvious what you're gonna do.

My oldest brother, Chester, he joined up first 'cause he figured he could get a decent pair of boots. So he walks twenty-five miles to goddamn Winnipeg to enlist, and arrives back home three days later in a brand new uniform and a shiny pair a boots on his feet. Well, that pretty much sold me and my other brother Marty, so me and Marty—we take turns borrowin' Chester 's boots to go and enlist. By the end of the week, there's the three of us, eh? Me, Marty and Chester, standin' on that porch together in our brand new uniforms and our shiny pairs a boots…

It wasn't patriotism that got us to join up. That "King and Country" bullshit went out after WWI. I tell ya, it was those goddamn boots! That and the fact that the Army was gonna pay us $1.10 a day. I was only makin' a buck a week on some damn farm I'd gotten work on.

The three of us was in the Artillery. We had no idea what we were gettin' ourselves into. But the truth is, we joined 'cause we knew we'd get hot meals, a trip to Europe and a shiny pair a boots.

ISABELLE: Grand-mama, can I please go and talk to him?

GRAND-MAMA: No Isabelle, you leave him alone.

JAKE: Goddamn it, I can't believe it's been sixty years. That's a long time. Well, I guess if you're dead at sixty it's not a long time, but if you're thinkin' about what ya did sixty years ago…

                I swore I'd never come back to this goddamn beach. My wife Marie bugged me about comin' back here, eh? And me and Marty fought about it all the time. He came back for the 40th anniversary, and the 50th, and he begged me to come with him, but I could never do it…

                Now that he's gone, I kinda wish I had. I guess I came back this time for him, for Marty, well, and Chester too. And a course you know, when the government said they were gonna give each veteran a thousand bucks to get over here, I didn't have no more excuses. Next thing I knew I was on a goddamn plane. Well, Marty, you won.

ISABELLE: Please, Grand-mama!

GRAND-MAMA: Isabelle, I said no! Don't you bother him with your questions about the war, mademoiselle.

ISABELLE: I won't! Sheesh…my grand-mama tells me not to do lots of things… But I do them anyway… (*Jumps off the bench towards JAKE.*) HI!

JAKE: AAHHH Jesus! Don't do that! What the hell are ya tryin' a do, give me a goddamn heart attack?!

ISABELLE: Sorry.

JAKE: Oh my god…

ISABELLE: What are you doing?

JAKE: What the hell does it look like I'm doin'?!

ISABELLE:	Mmmm, nothing.
JAKE:	That's what I'm doin'. Nothin'.
ISABELLE:	Oh. What's your name?
JAKE:	What's my...? Kid, ya just about scared the livin' daylights outta me. Do ya think I feel like givin' ya my name?
ISABELLE:	I said I was sorry, sheesh.
JAKE:	Didn't your parents ever tell ya not to talk to strangers?
ISABELLE:	Yeah, but you're not a stranger. My grand-mama and I saw you walking on the beach.
JAKE:	...You *saw* me walkin' on the beach? Kid, if that is your definition of "not a stranger" then you are in for some serious trouble.
ISABELLE:	Why?
JAKE:	...Oh my god. What's yer name?
ISABELLE:	I asked you first.
JAKE:	Heh, yeah, well that's pretty top-secret information, ya know. I dunno if I can give out that information to just anyone, especially someone who just about gave me a goddamn heart attack.
ISABELLE:	I'm not just anyone!
JAKE:	You're not, eh? Well, who are ya then?
ISABELLE:	I'm Isabelle.
JAKE:	Oh yeah? So. Who's Isabelle?
ISABELLE:	Isabelle is me! Everyone knows me. Well, not everyone, but most people.

JAKE: They do, do they? Well, you must be pretty special.

ISABELLE: Yeah, that's what my grand-mama says. She's called Isabelle too. She's grande-Isabelle and I'm petite-Isabelle. That's so no one mixes us up. But, um, I don't really understand that because I don't think it'd be too hard to know the difference. I'm ten. She's seventy. I think it's pretty obvious.

JAKE: Yeah, I'd probably have to agree with you there. You speak pretty good English for a French kid.

ISABELLE: Well, my papa was born in Ireland, so sometimes we speak English. My parents are there right now, but I didn't want to go because I wanted to stay here for the Anniversary. (*Making sure her grandmother isn't watching her.*)

                Mmm, my uh…my grand-mama says that you're one of the soldiers. Is that right?

JAKE: Yeah, that's right.

ISABELLE: Do you know what?

JAKE: …No, what?

ISABELLE: I have the most important job in the whole of the world.

JAKE: Really? Well, that sounds like a pretty big deal.

ISABELLE: Yeah, well, it's not *just* me; me and my classmates. We all take care of the soldiers. We clean their rooms for them and tidy their gardens because, well, they can't do it for themselves anymore.

JAKE: …Well, those are some lucky soldiers.

ISABELLE: Yeah, that's what my grand-mama says. So, you came here for the D-Day Anniversary?

JAKE: Yeah, I sure did.

ISABELLE:	Well, everyone's very happy that so many of you came back. Hey, do you like all the flags?
JAKE:	Yeah, that's quite a treat. God, I never seen that many Canadian flags flyin', even in Canada. Yep, that's quite somethin'.
ISABELLE:	Canada flags are always flying here. I like the Canada flag. I like that maple leaf in the middle. It's pretty. I wish I had a real maple leaf tree. My grand-mama says that some maple leaves turn that colour red in the autumn. Is that true?
JAKE:	That is certainly true.
ISABELLE:	Wow. That must be pretty.
JAKE:	Yeah, it's pretty pretty.
ISABELLE:	So, um, do you have any family here with you?
JAKE:	Uh…yeah, as a matter a fact I do. I got a brother here.
ISABELLE:	Really? Can I meet him too?
JAKE:	Well, no, you can't meet him. I mean, he's here, but…I mean he's buried at Bény-sur-Mer Cemetery.
ISABELLE:	Oh. I'm sorry.
JAKE:	Yeah, well. Me too.
ISABELLE:	Well, when was the last time that you came here?
JAKE:	This is the first time since the war.
ISABELLE:	(*Beat.*) You've *never* come back here to visit your brother?
JAKE:	No, I haven't.
ISABELLE:	Why?

JAKE: Look, kid. I would rather not talk about that, all right?

ISABELLE: Why?

JAKE: Because.

ISABELLE: Because why?

JAKE: Just because, all right?

ISABELLE: My papa says that "Because" is not an answer.

JAKE: Well, it's my answer!

ISABELLE: Well, what made you come back this time?

JAKE: Goddamnit! What the hell? Ya gotta know everyone else's business?

ISABELLE: No! Just trying to make conversation, sheesh.

JAKE: Ah, god. Look, if ya must know, I got another brother named Marty, all right?...I *had* another brother. He died not too long ago, and he was always pissed off at me for never comin' back over here with him to visit Chester—that's our brother that died here. So I guess it's my way of makin' it up to Marty, all right? And also, well, I knew this was my last chance really.

ISABELLE: Mmmm, you mean because you're so old.

JAKE: Yep. (*Beat.*) Thanks for remindin' me.

ISABELLE: You're welcome.

JAKE: Ah god...look, kid, let's just change the subject all right? You, um, I don't know...uh...do you know any jokes?

ISABELLE: Mmmm...not really. Do you?

JAKE: Knock-knock.

ISABELLE:	What kind of joke is that?
JAKE:	Not What. Who. Who's there? I say "knock-knock" and you say, "Who's there?"
ISABELLE:	Who's where?
JAKE:	Ah god, no. Look, kid, I am tryin' to tell ya a joke! A knock-knock joke? Ah my god, look, look. Look, I say knock-knock as if I was…uh…I don't know… ya know, like knockin' on a door or somethin', all right? Now you, you wanna find out who's behind that door. So you say, "Who's there?"
ISABELLE:	Oh… But why?
JAKE:	Because it's a joke! Don't ya have goddamn jokes in France?
ISABELLE:	Yeah, but…
JAKE:	Look, kid, do you wanna hear the goddamn joke or not?
ISABELLE:	Yeah, I want to hear the joke! Sheesh, you don't have to be so grumpy.
JAKE:	All right. Look. I am gonna say "knock-knock" and then you will say, "Who's there?"…Are you ready to try this now?
ISABELLE:	Yeah.
JAKE:	All right. Knock-knock.
ISABELLE:	Who's there?
JAKE:	Isabelle. Now you say, "Isabelle who?"
ISABELLE:	Isabelle who?!
JAKE:	Is-a-bell necessary on a bicycle? …Heh-heh, ya get it?! God, that one always cracks me up.

ISABELLE: Haaahhh, yeah, I get it. "Is a bell, ring, ring." That's
              funny.

JAKE: Oh my god, that was painful.

ISABELLE: I never heard my name in a joke before.

JAKE: Ahh, well, it's pretty important to have your name
              in a joke, ya know. Only real important people have
              their names in jokes.

ISABELLE: Really? Why?

JAKE: Well, it means ya got special powers, eh? You know,
              like uh, like magic powers.

ISABELLE: Wow, magic? Hey, that means my grand-mama is
              magic too.

JAKE: That's right. That's probably how she knew I was a
              soldier.

ISABELLE: Yeah, probably... Do you have your name in a joke?

JAKE: Well, no, but uh...my name is Jake, and that's only
              one letter away from joke so I got pretty special
              powers just by default.

ISABELLE: What kind of powers?

JAKE: Well, I'm a pretty good dancer, eh? In fact, in some
              circles they call me the "soft shoe king." I got some
              pretty good moves.

ISABELLE: Really? Can I see your moves?

JAKE: What, now?

ISABELLE: Yeah.

JAKE: Nah...I don't think so.

ISABELLE: Please?! Come on...

JAKE: Ah god…all right then, but ya better move outta my way though. I wouldn't wantcha to be blown away by my moves. Oh, by the way, since we're magic, we can summon up some music, all right? Hey Maestro! How 'bout some Frankie?

"You Make Me Feel So Young" by Frank Sinatra starts playing.

Can you hear that, Isabelle?

ISABELLE: Wow! Yeah, I can!

JAKE: See, I told ya! All right now, here we go, Izzy. Here we go. Watch the feet, watch and learn, watch and learn. *"You make me feel so spring has sprung."* All right now, we're gonna do some big fancy moves to the right. Are you ready? *"I'm such a happy individual."* (*JAKE does a not-so-steady move to the right as he sings the word "individual."*)

"The moment that you speak." One more this way. All right now, even it out to the left now, two to the left, two to the left. *"I'm gonna go and"*…ah… I don't remember the goddamn words but that doesn't matter. All right now… Now we're gonna come centre here for the biggest fanciest move that there is, are you ready for it? All right, hold onto your socks. Here we go… here we go…comin' up any second now… Ah god, nah, that's enough. Cut the music!

ISABELLE: Wow, Jake, that was neat! Do it again!

JAKE: Ah my god…no way, maybe later, all right?

ISABELLE: Where did you learn how to dance like that?!

JAKE: Ah…well, I guess Chester taught me how to dance. He taught me all sorts a stuff about music. He introduced me to Frankie, and god, he could cut a rug like nobody's business... In fact, uh, well, ya know, before we made our way over here, we spent most of our days off in England dancin' our hearts out. That was the best damn part of the war.

ISABELLE: Soldiers know how to dance?

JAKE: You betcha. Well, there were a ton of us you know; eighteen, nineteen, twenty years old with nothin' to do but wait to get over here. So, they opened up the opera houses and the dance halls at 10 o'clock in the mornin', and they kept 'em open all day and night, eh? (*After 10 o'clock in the mornin' Benny Goodman's "We'll Meet Again" starts to softly underscore, and JAKE starts to imagine the orchestra and the dance halls.*)

There were big fancy orchestras playin' and tiny bands too. Chester played in one of them tiny bands a few times. He was one mean trumpet player.

ISABELLE: Chester played the trumpet in a real live band?

JAKE: He sure did.

ISABELLE: Wow.

JAKE: Yeah well, I got to know him better in them England dance halls than I ever did at home.

Somethin' about playin' that trumpet just transformed Chester. It was like his third arm or somethin'. I never saw him without it— people cheerin' for him, girls goin' crazy over him. (*Beat. Music fades out.*) Yep, England was one hell of a hurrah.

I think we just danced our feet off 'cause we knew we were goin' some place we might not come back from.

ISABELLE:	Who did you dance with?
JAKE:	Ah, you know, the local girls would come out and spend their days dancin' with us. Lotsa the guys met their wives in them dance halls—the War Brides—much to the chagrin of the girlfriends at home.
ISABELLE:	Did you have a favourite song to dance to?
JAKE:	Yep, all the slow ones.
ISABELLE:	Why?
JAKE:	Uh...never mind... I didn't have no particular favourite, but because I liked the slow stuff I'd have to say I had a bit of a soft spot for old Vera. You know..."

"We'll meet again..."

Sound cue of Vera Lynn's "We'll Meet Again." JAKE starts to sing along and gets caught up in his dance hall memories. He slow dances with an imaginary partner and after the lyric "keep smiling through" he breaks out of his reverie.

God, we must a heard that goddamn song a million times. Some of the guys hated hearin' it 'cause they didn't goddamn believe it. But me? I just liked the fact that I got to dance close to some pretty girl. (*Music fades out.*) Everyone wanted their own Vera Lynn.

Chester coulda had his pick of any girl in them dance halls, but he already had his own Vera back home. He wrote to her all the time, eh? She was real nice to me, treated me like her kid brother right from the start. On the worst days over here that's what got a lot a guys through, eh? Gettin' back to Vera, whoever that was for each of us, our own Vera Lynns.

ISABELLE:	Do you have a Vera?

JAKE: As a matter of fact I do. Her name's Marie. We were
                married for fifty-seven years, but uh...well, she
                died a few years ago.

ISABELLE: Oh. Do you miss her?

JAKE: ...Every day. (*Beat.*) I...uh...well, ya know, I still
                write to her, ya know.

ISABELLE: You do? But...umm, where do you send the letters?

JAKE: Well, can you keep a secret?

ISABELLE: Mmm, not really.

JAKE: Oh my god... Well, I'll tell ya anyway. Me and
                Marie, we got a favourite bench down at the end of
                our garden, eh? Now, I put a secret compartment
                under that bench with a lock and two keys; one for
                her and one for me, and that is where we left letters
                for one another.

ISABELLE: Wow, Jake, that's neat.

JAKE: Yeah...well, I still put letters there for her sometimes
                and a course, ya know, I go down there to talk to
                her.

ISABELLE: Does she talk back?

JAKE: Well, no, but I'd have to say she's a pretty good
                listener.

                So, petite Isabelle, don't you think you should be
                gettin' home soon? I mean, won't your grandma be
                worried about ya?

ISABELLE: No, that's OK. I just live in that house right over
                there.

JAKE: (*Beat.*) Really? ...You live in that house, eh? I
                remember that house.

ISABELLE: You do?

JAKE:	Sure I do. That was the first house that was liberated on D-Day. Queen's Own Rifles; first boys to hit this part of the beach… (*Beat*.) You live there, eh?
ISABELLE:	Yeah. It's the most famous house in Normandy… Well, maybe not Normandy, but lots of soldiers remember it from the war.
	My grand-mama had to move out of it when the Nazi soldiers came. She was my age when you came here. She's sad sometimes. Her papa was killed by a Nazi soldier.
JAKE:	I see. Well, that's kinda young to have to go through somethin' like that.
ISABELLE:	Yeah… Hey, Jake, well, um, do you know the Burlington Teen Tour Band?
JAKE:	What the hell? No, can't say as I do.
ISABELLE:	Well, I bet Chester knows them since he's a trumpet player! They're a marching band from Burlington, Ontario. I like to say that; On-tario-o! They're all just kids like me, and they're going to play at the ceremony tomorrow at Bény-Sur-Mer Cemetery *and* on June 6th here on the beach. I watched them practice on the beach this morning. I want to do that when I get bigger. I want to play in the Burlington Teen Tour Band!
JAKE:	Ya do, do ya? Well, do you play any instruments? Maybe you could sneak up on the beach and play with them.
ISABELLE:	No, I only know how to play the recorder.
JAKE:	Yeah, well, I guess there's not much call for a recorder in a marching band, but that's a good start though. I mean ya gotta start somewhere, right? Maybe one day you can play with them.
ISABELLE:	Do you think so?

JAKE: Well, god, I don't know! Maybe. Ya know, if ya practice.

ISABELLE: Yeah, maybe... Hey, Jake, what's that written on your hand?

JAKE: ...(*Looking at the palm of his hand.*)...X E 10.

ISABELLE: What does that mean?

JAKE: That is a...uh...a secret code I gotta remember.

ISABELLE: What's it for?

JAKE: Well if I tell ya that it won't be much of a secret anymore, now will it?

ISABELLE: I guess not. But...umm, I won't tell.

JAKE: Ya just finished tellin' me ya can't keep a secret!

ISABELLE: Fine!... Hey, Jake? Do you know what my favourite number is?

JAKE: ...Now what the hell do I look like, a psychic? Of course I don't know what your favourite number is.

ISABELLE: It is...two thousand and forty-eight.

JAKE: (*Beat.*) What the hell kind of favourite number is that? 2048? I mean, most people choose one digit or two—but four? That is just weird.

ISABELLE: Yeah well, I'm not most people.

JAKE: Oo-ooohhh, heh-heh... Touché!

ISABELLE: Hahh, I didn't know that you spoke French! Aaahh...

JAKE: Aaahh, smart-ass. So petite Isabelle, why is 2048 your favourite number?

ISABELLE: Because that's the number of soldiers that are buried at Bény-Sur-Mer Cemetery.

JAKE: (*Beat.*) Ah yeah…right…well, that's…that's a good favourite number. Listen, kid, I gotta get goin' here, all right? Now you, uh, you should probably get home too.

ISABELLE: Oh, no…but don't…uh…don't you want to come to my house for dinner? You could meet my grand-mama.

JAKE: Look, kid, that's nice of you, all right, but I got some, uh… some stuff I gotta take care of.

ISABELLE: What kind of stuff?

JAKE: The kind of stuff that is none of your business.

ISABELLE: All right. Well, are you going to be at the cemetery tomorrow?

JAKE: Yeah, I'll be there. I gotta find Chester.

ISABELLE: Me too, I'll be there. Then maybe I can help you look for him.

JAKE: Yeah, maybe, all right? But just, maybe.

ISABELLE: Oh. OK. Well, bye, Jake. See you tomorrow.

JAKE: See ya… (*Watches her run home.*)…petite Isabelle… Look, kid, maybe you could help me… nah… just forget it.

> *JAKE watches ISABELLE's home a little bit longer and then he slowly scans left across the beach, remembering the D-Day landing.*

…God…

> *JAKE walks stage left to the side table, the lights change and we are now in JAKE's hotel room. He notices something going on outside his window. He leans over the side table and peers out.*

What the? …Ah, jeeze…

JAKE sees other veterans gathering outside. He wonders whether or not he should join them. After a few moments, he picks up the small black typewriter case next to the side table and places it on top of the side table. He opens the case, which contains his Legion uniform meticulously kept. JAKE looks in the mirror as he dresses [the mirror is invisible, downstage and facing the audience]. He dusts off his Legion jacket. It is decorated with his campaign medals. He struggles to put the jacket on.

Ah...come on.

Once the jacket is on JAKE turns back to the side table and picks up a poppy from inside the case. He struggles to put the poppy on the left lapel of his jacket. Once the poppy is on, he turns back to the side table to get his beret out of the case. Once the beret is securely on, he adjusts his artillery tie, which he is already wearing. He stares into the mirror and after a few seconds he starts to see himself as a young soldier. He slowly stands tall for the first time and salutes. After a few seconds, he returns to his stooped posture, and stares at himself in the mirror, an old man once again. He walks centre stage. The lights change.

Part 2 – Bény-Sur-Mer Cemetery

JAKE: They got us shuttle buses to the cemetery. I talked to guys I hadn't seen in sixty years. Fred Rogers, Jan De Vries, Art Heximer, Al Mason, Bill Rowe. A great buncha guys I wished I'd kept in touch with.

We got on the buses and drove past the old fields I remember fightin' in. And then, in what seemed like the middle of nowhere, we came up to this nest of tall trees, all swayin' in the breeze, and then the bus stopped. We were at Bény-Sur-Mer Cemetery. I was gonna see Chester.

A lot of the guys got choked up when we made our way through the entrance. A lot hadn't been back for a long time, if ever, just like me. And it was a sight to walk in and see how peaceful it was, so different from the last time. And there, right in front of us, were all our buddies, row, after row, after row. (*Beat.*) And you can't help but think, "Why wasn't it me?"

I was feeling kinda nervous about seein' Chester, but a bit excited too, like it was time. I started lookin' for him. (*JAKE looks and reads the inscription on his hand as he scans the graveyard.*) Plot X, Row E, Grave 10.

ISABELLE: Grand-mama and I rode our bicycles to Bény-Sur-Mer, and a lot of buses passed us on the way, all full of veterans. We waved to them as they passed by. They waved back and smiled. It was nice to see them so happy. And somewhere, on one of those buses, was the Burlington Teen Tour Band.

When we got to the cemetery there were lots of people there already, a lot more than usual. Before the ceremony started I wanted to say hi to the soldiers I take care of. I ran over to where they were, but when I got there, there was a lady already talking to one of them. It made me kind of mad.

Excuse me? What are you doing at my grave?

SUSAN: Your grave? Well, my dear, you seem alive and well to me.

ISABELLE: Well, I don't mean my grave. I just mean that I take care of this soldier. (*Pointing to the grave.*) Well, he's *one* of the soldiers I take care of.

SUSAN: (*Beat.*) Well, isn't that sweet of you. And what's your name?

Julia Mackey as Jake.

Photo by Tim Matheson.

ISABELLE: Isabelle.

SUSAN: That's a pretty name. My name's Susan. I'm a teacher from Canada. Now, I was just putting this maple leaf on the grave as a thank you from one of my students. My students made them for the veterans. Some I've given directly to the veterans, and some I'm putting on the graves like this one.

ISABELLE: (*Beat.*) Is that a real live maple leaf from Canada?!

SUSAN: Well, no, it's not real. It's made of red paper and then we just put plastic on it. You know—so it doesn't get ruined if it rains.

ISABELLE: Can I see that maple leaf?

SUSAN: Of course you can.

ISABELLE: (*To the audience.*) I picked up the maple leaf and held it there for a while. It was the same exact size as my hand. It was bright red, just like the one on the flag, and it had some writing on it and a picture of a boy. He was cute.

             Who's this boy?

SUSAN: His name is Danny Brown, and he's a very good student of mine back home in Ontario.

ISABELLE: ON-TARIO?! Do you know the Burlington Teen Tour Band?

SUSAN: Well, of course I do. They're playing here today. Do you know them too?

ISABELLE: Yes. No. Kind of. I watched them practise on the beach. Can I keep this maple leaf?

SUSAN: …Well, Isabelle…I know that Danny would be very flattered to know that you want his maple leaf, but I also know he'd very much like the soldier to have it. (*Pointing at the grave.*)

Why don't you just leave it here, and you can take
care of it when you come visit here.

ISABELLE: Sure, I can do that. (*Reading the maple leaf.*) *"I think
you're great for helping make Canada a peaceful country,
Je me souviens."* Did Danny write that?

SUSAN: He sure did.

ISABELLE: That's nice. (*Beat.*) Can I write to him?

SUSAN: Um, Well, I don't...see why not. I tell you what;
you can tell him that his maple leaf is on one of the
graves you take care of. I bet he would love to know
that.

ISABELLE: And so she gave me her address, and I'm going
to write to Danny Brown, who will most certainly
become my boyfriend after that. Especially once he
knows that I know about the Burlington Teen Tour
Band from ON-TARIOOO! Speaking of boyfriends,
I was about to tell Grand-mama about the maple
leaf when I saw Jake walking close by.

Jake! Hi, Jake!

JAKE: Eh! Look who it is! Petite Isabelle! How are ya?

ISABELLE: Good. Hey, Jake, did you find Chester yet?

JAKE: No, not yet. I just got here.

ISABELLE: Oh. Well, Jake, I want to introduce you to the
soldiers I take care of.

JAKE: They're here?

ISABELLE: Yeah, they're right over there. Come on.

JAKE: No, no, no. Look, Isabelle, I really gotta look for
Chester first. Maybe I can meet up with them later,
all right?

ISABELLE: Please? Come on!

JAKE: Ah god...all right then...well, hold on a sec. Hold on a sec!

ISABELLE runs stage left and points at the graves as she mentions their names.

ISABELLE: Jake, this is Mr. Smith and this is M. Pelletier. Now, they're fighting because Mr. Smith's roses keep making M. Pelletier sneeze.

And this is Mr. Hebner. I like his inscription the best. *"He has gone across the river, whose shores are evergreen, ever remembered by Mother and the rest of the family. Riding Park, Manitoba."*

...Jake? What's the matter?

JAKE: ...My mother wrote that. (*Beat.*) God, Isabelle, when you told me you take care of the soldiers, I thought you were talkin' about some old folks' home or somethin'. I didn't know ya meant the graves.

ISABELLE looks at JAKE and then at Chester's grave. She is amazed that Chester is one of the soldiers she takes care of.

ISABELLE   Yeah...that's what I meant. Me and my classmates. That's our job. We take care of them because, well, because they died for our freedom, so far away from their own homes, and because their own families live too far away to do it for them.

Grand-mama says, "You must clean their rooms, Isabelle, take care of their gardens and pull out all the weeds so that they can see through their windows." (*She points to M. Pelletier's grave in front of her.*) ...Jake, I like that Chester 's one of the soldiers I take care of.

JAKE: Yeah well, I like that you take care of Chester too. You're a better friend to him than I ever was.

ISABELLE: That's not true.

JAKE: Sure it is.

ISABELLE: I don't think he thinks that. Are you going to talk to
                him?

JAKE: What are you, crazy? No, I am not gonna talk to
                him. He's dead.

ISABELLE: Well, Marie's dead and you talk to her don't you?

JAKE: Of course I talk to Marie! But that is different! She's
                Marie. I was married to her for fifty-seven years. I
                know her. I know what to say!

ISABELLE: It's not different. You just know her better, that's all.
                You don't have to be afraid.

JAKE: I am *not* afraid.

ISABELLE: Sure you are. I'd be afraid if I were you. You haven't
                talked to your brother in *sixty* years! That's a really
                long time to go without talking to your brother.
                Mmmm…I got an idea. Why don't you just pretend
                that you're on the phone?

JAKE: I hate the goddamn phone.

ISABELLE: Oh. Well…I got another idea. You don't gotta say
                anything. You can just sit here with him, and then
                he'll know that you're here and that you care about
                him. Well, that's what I do sometimes.

JAKE: …Ah yeah? How'd ya get so smart?

ISABELLE: Well, it's just the way I was borned I guess. Hey,
                Jake, I'm going to go find my grand-mama so that
                you can talk to Chester.

JAKE: No, you don't gotta leave.

ISABELLE: Yes, I do.

JAKE:	Wait!
ISABELLE:	Bye…
JAKE:	Goddammit… (*Beat.*) …all these people around…

JAKE looks around, feeling self-conscious. He walks over and sits on the bench. After a few seconds he speaks, initially conscious of all the people around.

Hey, Chester. How's Marty doin'? Say hi to him for me. Tell him he still owes me twenty bucks.

Listen. I told that kid Isabelle that I came back here to make it up to Marty, you know? But that's not true. I came back here to make it up to you. I wanna tell ya how sorry I am I never came back here to visit ya. I always thought about it, but I just wanted to remember you in them dance halls, not some goddamn grave.

It wasn't right, you know. You bein' stuck over here while me and Marty got to live out our lives at home. I wish I coulda traded places with ya. You had somethin' real special, you know, that you coulda done with your music. Me? I never done nothin' special.

But I've tried to live a good life for ya. And I wantcha to know that not a goddamn day goes by when I don't think about ya.

The day the war ended, we were in some farmhouse, and it came over the tannoy, "Empty guns, cease fire."…The war was over. No one said nothin', eh? No whoopin' or hollerin' like there was back home. We just lay there in bed, and no one said a goddamn word.

After me and Marty got back home, we hoped every day they'd made a mistake. I don't know, we thought maybe somehow you just got lost or somethin'. And one day you'd come walkin' through that front door…wearin' those goddamn boots, and I'd hand you over your trumpet, all shined up and ready to go, eh? (*Beat.*) But you never did.

I'm glad that kid Isabelle's been takin' good care of ya. God, she's a bit of a nut, but then so were you, so I guess that fits. She's been a better friend to you than I ever was and for that I'm truly sorry.

I hope you can forgive me for takin' so long to come visit ya. I sure missed not havin' ya around.

Overwhelmed, JAKE starts to cry silently.

ISABELLE: Hi Jake.

JAKE: Hey, Isabelle. How's it goin'?

JAKE reaches for a hanky in his pocket and tries to hide that he's been crying from ISABELLE.

ISABELLE: Good. The ceremony's about to start. The Burlington Teen Tour Band's gonna play. Can I sit with you?

JAKE: Uh…yeah, yeah, sure you can.

ISABELLE: Did you have a nice chat with Chester?

JAKE: Yes, yes I did, thanks.

ISABELLE: (*ISABELLE leans forward to see that JAKE has been crying.*) Um…Jake…um…my grand-mama says that when you lose someone you love, that pain never goes away, and some days it sits so close to your heart that you can't help but to cry. (*Beat.*) I'm glad that you talked to Chester.

JAKE: Yeah well, me too. (*Beat.*) Look kid…just…just thanks, all right?… God… (*Managing to look at her.*) Thanks.

JAKE struggles to get up from the bench. He looks at Chester's grave, and then slowly walks to the next few graves ISABELLE had pointed to and reads their headstones. M. Pelletier, Mr. Smith. He scans the graveyard and recites "The Act of Remembrance."

They shall grow not old, as we that are left grow old: Age shall not weary them, nor the years condemn. At the going down of the sun and in the morning we will remember them.

Part 3 – Return to Juno

ISABELLE: The next day was June 6th, D-Day! Grand-mama and I made our way down early to Juno beach. We wanted to make sure we had a good seat for the ceremony, and I wanted to see if I could see Jake.

There were some really important people there, all wearing funny hats and making nice speeches about what the veterans did and how important the Canadians were to French liberation. The veterans were very happy.

And then everything got quiet, like people were just waiting for something to happen...

Sound Cue: A lone bagpiper playing "The Flowers of the Forest."

And then all you could hear was the sound of one bagpiper playing on the beach. No one said anything, people just watched. And then one by one, the veterans started to march back together down to the beach. And as they did, the Burlington Teen Tour Band joined the piper, and they played until every last veteran had returned to Juno Beach.

Julia Mackey as Isabelle and Jake.
Photo by Tim Matheson.

As they marched by, people clapped and cheered and said, "Thank you! Merci!" and Grand-mama and I waved and cheered too. And when they were all gathered on the beach, some just stood and chatted with an old friend, and I even saw one man take something out of his pocket and throw it into the water. And some walked right down to the water and stared out at it for a long time.

Why are they staring Grand-mama?

GRAND-MAMA: Because they are remembering, Isabelle.

ISABELLE: Their friends?

GRAND-MAMA: Yes, their friends, and other things too perhaps.

ISABELLE: Oh...

Grand-mama, I think that I see Jake. Jake?! Over here, Jake! Over here!

JAKE: Hey, look who it is! Petite Isabelle! How are ya?

ISABELLE: Good. Jake, this is my grand-mama.

JAKE: Well, Grande-Isabelle, it's nice to finally meet ya.

GRAND-MAMA: Jake, it's a pleasure to meet you. Isabelle has been talking about you non-stop. Im so glad she got a chance to meet you.

JAKE: Ah, I was lucky to meet her. She told me about you too. I'm a...I'm sorry about what happened to your father.

GRAND-MAMA: And I'm sorry about your brother.

JAKE: Yeah, well, I guess sometimes we gotta lose one thing to win somethin' else.

GRAND-MAMA: I know, and I thank you so much for that.

JAKE: Yeah well, I figure I done somethin' pretty good
                 with my life after all, eh? Comin' here all them years
                 ago?

GRAND-MAMA: I would say so.

ISABELLE: Hey Jake, when are you going home?

JAKE: Well, me and some of the guys are gonna catch a
                 train to Pa-ree tomorrow mornin', and then I'm
                 flying home from there.

ISABELLE: Oh…that's too soon.

JAKE: Yeah. I'm afraid so.

ISABELLE: Hey, there's a café in front of the train station. I
                 could meet you there for coffee before you go. I
                 want to give you something.

JAKE: Aren't you a little bit young to be drinkin' coffee?

ISABELLE: Jake. I'm French. I can drink what I want.

JAKE: Oh, well excusez-moi. Well then, yes, petite
                 Isabelle, I would be honoured to meetcha for *un café*
                 tomorrow.

ISABELLE: Great. Well, bye Jake, see you tomorrow.

JAKE: See ya. (*Beat.*) Grand-Isabelle, it was a pleasure
                 meetin' ya.

GRAND-MAMA: Jake…that pleasure was all mine.

                 *ISABELLE turns to her grandmother, as she hears
                 the emotion in her grandmother's voice.*

ISABELLE: …So the next day I met Jake at the train station.

                 Hey Jake, I have that present for you.

JAKE: Ah god, you didn't have to go gettin' me a present,
                 but uh, well, thank you very much. You want that
                 I should open it now?

ISABELLE:	Yeah.
JAKE:	All right then, let's take a look see here. Wow…it's uh…it's dirt.
ISABELLE:	Jake! It's not just *any* dirt. It's dirt from Chester's garden. (*Pointing down to indicate his grave.*) I thought that maybe you could put it in your garden at home, and then you could plant something in that exact same spot and then whatever grows there could be Chester, and you could talk to him every day. It could be like your very own gravestone for him but at home.
JAKE:	(*Beat.*) Isabelle, that's lovely of you. I will do that for sure. And I'll tell him it was your idea, all right? Now, before I get goin' here, I want you to give me your address, and one of these days, ya might find something in the mail, for you, from me, at no expense to you.
ISABELLE:	What?
JAKE:	Well, it's a bit of a present for you too.
ISABELLE:	A present for me?! What is it?!
JAKE:	Well if I tell ya that, it won't be much of a present anymore now will it?
ISABELLE:	No, I guess not…
JAKE:	All right then. (*Beat.*) Well, Isabelle necessary on a bike? I gotta catch a train… You…you be good to your Grandma, all right? And thanks for taking care of Chester. And you keep practicing that recorder, ya promise?
ISABELLE:	I promise. (*Beat.*) I'll miss you Jake…I don't want you to go home. I love you.

JAKE: Now you cut that out, goddamn it. Look uh...look, I'll call ya all right?

ISABELLE: But you hate the goddamn phone.

JAKE: Oh my god...well, I will call you anyway all right? (*Beat.*) Look kid, I really gotta get goin' here. I'll see ya. Petite Isabelle.

ISABELLE: Bye Jake. ...Bye Jake!...BYE Jake!

               I waved to Jake as I watched him enter the train station and disappear into the crowd of veterans... all heading home. (*Pause.*)

               Then I rode my bicycle home and told Grand-mama about what Jake had said about sending me a present. It was ages and ages before the present *finally* arrived. Every day I asked my Grand-mama about it and every day she said,

GRAND-MAMA: Mon Dieu, Isabelle! You have to learn to be patient.

ISABELLE: I am being patient! Sheesh.

               And then, one morning? I walked into the kitchen, and there was a brown box with a white envelope on it? And it had MY name on it! I was so excited, I ripped it open and started reading.

ISABELLE: Dear,

JAKE: Isabelle. So here it is, that present I told you about.

               Now before you go openin' it, just hold on a sec. I gotta few things I wanna tell ya first.

               First, I wanna tell ya I used that dirt you gave me. I planted a maple tree for Chester. Ah...you know, I thought you might like that. It's still a tiny thing, but it's growin' every day.

               Second, I want you to thank your grandmother for me for teaching you about the war. It um...well, it means a lot when someone young understands what it was we were tryin' to do, and that their lives might not a been so nice if the goddamn thing had failed.

Ah, I think you're one of the smartest kids I've ever met, eh? Ah, you're young yet, I mean you're gonna go through some rough spots, but don't let it get you down, eh? Everybody can't be perfect. Whatever it is, just say, "Well, this is terrible." Accept it. Don't moan and cry about it.

I got no doubt that you're gonna get to some pretty cool places in your lifetime. God…maybe even *Burlington, Ontario.*

Now, at the bottom of that box I sent ya, just underneath the present, there's two plastic bags of dirt. I want ya to take 'em, and I want you to scatter them on Chester's grave. One is dirt from Marty's grave, and the second is from mine. (*Beat.*)

Now, don't go gettin' all misty eyed on me. I didn't want some stranger telling you I was dead. I wanted to do that myself…

…So, I asked my buddy Jerry to pack up all this stuff for me, and send it on to you after I was gone.

This present is my way of thanking you for taking care of Chester. He and I talked about it, and he thought it was a pretty good idea too.

So, one last thing, all right? You take the present down to Juno Beach, don't open it 'til you get there. Find your favourite spot. You'll know what to do.

So long petite Isabelle. It was great meetin' ya…

> *JAKE winks goodbye and walks over to the side table. JAKE slowly takes off his jacket. He folds it carefully and places it back into the case. He removes*

his beret and sets it on top of the jacket. He puts on the cap he was originally wearing and closes the case. He taps the case lightly and then walks back to centre stage.

We'll meet again. Don't know where, don't know when, but I *know* we'll meet again some sunny day. Love,

ISABELLE: Jake.

ISABELLE stands still for a moment taking in the letter. She looks out to the audience, vulnerable. After a moment, she walks over to the bench and she picks up the parcel behind it. She walks back downstage centre.

I took Jake's present and ran as quick as I could to the beach. I went to the exact same spot where I first saw Jake staring out at the water, and I didn't open it 'til I got there.

ISABELLE sinks to the floor. She stares at the present for a moment and then opens it. It is filled with bright red maple leaves. She slowly scoops up as many leaves as she can, admiring them and JAKE's thoughtful gesture.

She throws the leaves up in the air. As they fall around her she notices another object in the box. She freezes, staring into the box, and then stands as she pulls JAKE's gift out of the box. It is Chester's trumpet.

She looks up to the sky, deeply moved by JAKE's gift.

ISABELLE: Thank you, Jake...

Now? Every June 6th, I come down to the beach with Jake's gift, and I remember Jake and Chester and Marty, and my great-grandfather, and all the men and women who died so that we might be free. To them I say, "Merci pour ma liberté. Je me souviendrai. I *will* remember."

Sound Cue: "The Last Post."

My name is Isabelle, and I have the most important job in the *whole* of the world.

ISABELLE looks up to the sky and gives a wink to JAKE. She scans the sky and then bows her head, holding the trumpet tightly. "The Last Post" continues getting louder as the lights slowly fade to black.

The End.

Julia Mackey as Isabelle.

Photo by Tim Matheson.

Danny Brown's maple leaf card keeps a watchful eye over Chester Hebner's grave, located at X E 10 in Bény-sur-Mer Cemetery, Normandy, France. June 5th, 2004. Photo by Julia Mackey.

Julia was drawn to Chester Hebner's grave when she noticed a red maple leaf card leaning up against the gravestone. When she turned the card over, the inscription read, "I think you're great for helping make Canada a peaceful country. Je me souviens." It was signed, Danny Brown. Danny's school in small-town Ontario was also listed on the card under his name. Julia found the school and discovered that a teacher named Susan had travelled to Normandy with her husband for the 60th Anniversary ceremonies. Before her travels, Susan had her students make red maple leaf thank you cards. When she arrived in Normandy, Susan placed some of the cards on graves and some she gave to veterans who had returned for the anniversary. Julia sent this photo and a letter with information about Chester Hebner to Danny Brown at his school so that he could see where his maple leaf card ended up and with which soldier. They have never met, but one day Julia hopes to meet Susan and Danny Brown in person.

Julia Mackey and Arthur Heximer meet on Juno Beach, June 6th, 2004. Photo by June Heximer.

After the main 60th Anniversary Ceremony at Juno Beach Centre was over, Julia saw a veteran standing alone next to one of the memorials on Juno Beach. When Julia approached Art he initially thought she was French as she was quite emotional when thanking him for his service. She explained she was Canadian and had made the journey to witness and be part of the 60th Anniversary Ceremonies. They chatted for a while, and before saying goodbye, Art's daughter, June Heximer, took this photo for Julia. When Julia returned to Canada she regretted not getting Art's address. She could remember that his first name was Arthur and that he lived in Mississauga, Ontario. iPhoto enabled Julia to blow up the photo so that she could clearly read Art's name tag, which displayed the last name Heximer. Julia then looked up all the A. Heximers in Mississauga, Ontario. She found three listings and wrote to all three. She sent them this photo with a letter addressed to Mr. A. Heximer. On the back of the envelope she wrote, "This letter is intended for Arthur Heximer, who I met on Juno Beach, June 6th, 2004 at the 60th Anniversary of D-Day." All three A. Heximers responded. The first response was from a young woman who had heard of Art but was not related to him. The second was from an elderly woman whose husband, Arnold Heximer, had been a WW2 veteran and had passed away ten years earlier. The last response was an email from Art confirming that he was indeed the Arthur she had met on Juno Beach. Julia and Art have had many visits since that first meeting in 2004. Julia and Dirk Van Stralen have become great friends with the Heximer family. They keep in touch to this day. Art served in the Canadian Army from 1942 until 1970. During WW2 he was a Corporal with the 1st Echelon 21st Army Group. Upon returning to Canada in 1946, Art served in the Royal Canadian Army Service Corps (RCASC) as a Sergeant and then Staff Sergeant at Base Borden.

Skyhawk Paratroopers salute a veteran on Juno Beach at the 60th Anniversary of D-Day ceremony in Normandy, France, June 6th, 2004. Photo by Julia Mackey.

In the right place at the right time. Julia snapped this photo right after the official D-Day ceremony at Juno Beach was coming to an end. These four Skyhawk paratroopers had just parachuted onto the beach moments before. Their parachutes were designed to look like Canadian flags. After they landed, they marched in unison down the beach, stopped in front of this veteran and saluted. When Julia and Dirk first started to tour *Jake's Gift*, they wanted the promotional material image to be of a veteran looking out over the shores of Juno Beach. This is the original photo that Dirk Van Stralen used to create that image, which is also the cover of this book.